Kermit
Learns
Windows

Starring Jim Henson's Muppets™

by Kathleen Resnick
Illustrations by Matthew Fox
Computer color by Tasa Graphic Arts, Inc.

PRIMA

Muppet Press

Well, hi there! I was just about to go into the after-school center to play with my friends. Can you see them through the window? They're already busy having fun. There's Piggy painting, Fozzie writing jokes, Gonzo playing games, and Skeeter adding up our club dues.

2

You know, Scooter showed me a window sort of like this one. You can do all kinds of different things in it. It even has a sign like this one. Come on inside. I'll show you!

Here it is! It's a window on the computer!

You know how there are a lot of different windows in a building? Well, there are also a lot of different windows on the computer. You can draw, paint, write, play games, and do many more things in them. But with all of these different windows, how do you keep them straight?

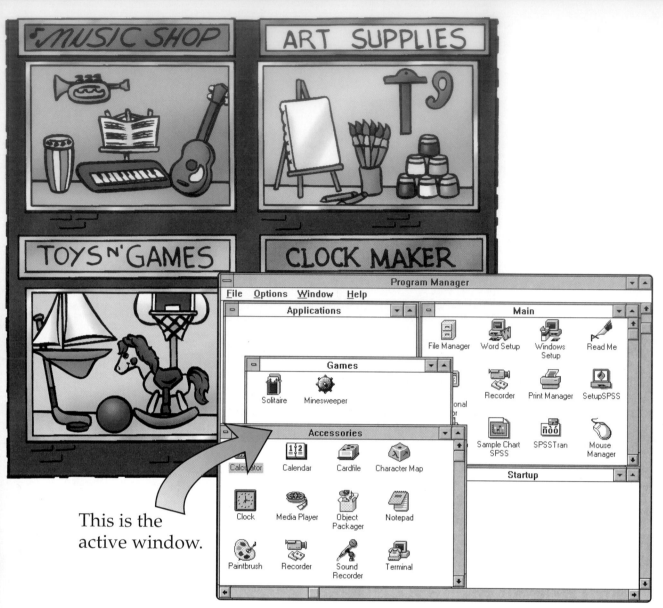

This is the active window.

It's easy, because every window has a sign. They're like the signs you see in store windows. See the bar on the top of each computer window? That's the window's sign. It's called a **title bar**. It tells you the name of the window, just as a store window sign tells you the name of the store. And the brightest title bar tells you which window you're working in. It's called the **active window**.

The tiny pictures in computer windows are called **icons**. An icon is a picture that stands for something. We sometimes use icons instead of words. They are found all around us, even in our computers.

Accessories

Paintbrush

Clock

If you can't figure out what an icon in a computer window stands for, you just have to look underneath it. Its name is right there.

Accessories

The **Accessories group icon** holds things that make your computer fun

Main

The **Main group icon** holds things that help you organize

Applications

The **Applications group icon** holds things that help you do your work

Games

The **Games group icon** holds games that are lots of fun to pl

There are two kinds of icons in computer windows. One kind is called a **group icon**. Group icons look like tiny windows that have even tinier icons in them. Group icons all look the same, except that each one has its own name printed under it.

The other kind of icon is called an **application icon**. Application icons stand for **programs**. You use programs to do things—like write a report for school, draw pictures, or add and subtract numbers. See the application icon that looks like a pen? That stands for a program called **Write**. You can use it to write letters to your friends. The icon that looks like paint and a brush is for the Paintbrush program. I use it all the time to draw and paint nifty pictures. Can you spot the **Calculator**, **Calendar**, and **Clock** icons?

Write

Calculator

Paintbrush

Calendar

Clock

A group icon is like a special trunk where I put away all my things. And they're always there waiting for me when I want to use them again! If I open a group icon I'll find the programs I want to use on my computer.

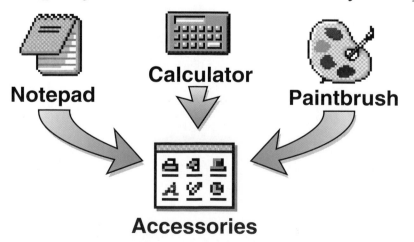

Notepad Calculator Paintbrush

Accessories

I want to show you a few more things about these icons. But first I need to tell you about something else. It's called a **mouse**. No, it's not that kind of a mouse, but it can be just as much fun! It doesn't have whiskers or fur and it doesn't live in a mouse hole, but it does have a tail and it sits on a **mouse pad**. It also has two, sometimes three, buttons on its back. When you press the **left button**, that's called **clicking** it. And clicking is one way to tell the computer what to do.

There's something else about the mouse. See the arrow on the screen? It's called a **pointer**. When I move the mouse on the mouse pad, the pointer on the screen moves, too. So if I move the mouse up, the pointer moves up. The pointer does exactly what I make the mouse do. Pretty neat, huh? You can use it to point to anything on the screen!

Scooter's Computer Tutor

Hey, why don't you try moving your mouse? Put your hand on the mouse and gently move the mouse around the pad. Can you make the arrow point to different icons? Good!

Now watch what happens when I move the pointer on the screen to a group icon and click once on the left mouse button. See the box that appears? It's called a **menu**. It gives you lots of choices, just the way a menu in a restaurant does. If I just click on the icon again, it's gone!

Remember, group icons look like little windows. *Only* group icons have menus—application icons don't.

Do you know what's really neat? **Double-clicking** on an icon. Just point the arrow on the screen to an icon and quickly click the left mouse button two times. (Make sure the arrow *touches* the icon.) Let's try it on the **Accessories** icon!

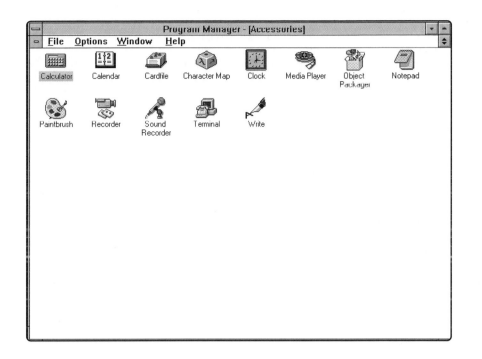

Ta dah! A new window appears! Hey, the window's name in the title bar is the same as the group icon's name I just clicked on. And look at all the application icons in the group window we just opened. Let's practice our double-clicking on a few more group icons and see what happens.

Scooter's Computer Tutor

Double-clicking is tricky. But don't worry—you'll get the hang of it! If a new window doesn't appear when you double-click, try again. If a menu pops up, just click once on the first choice in the menu . . . the word **Restore**. You just learned another way to open a group window.

15

Oh boy, look at all the windows I have open at once. What a mess! Does your screen look like this, too? Let's clean up this clutter and close these windows.

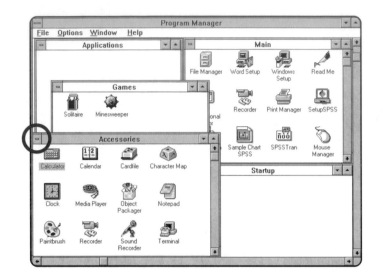

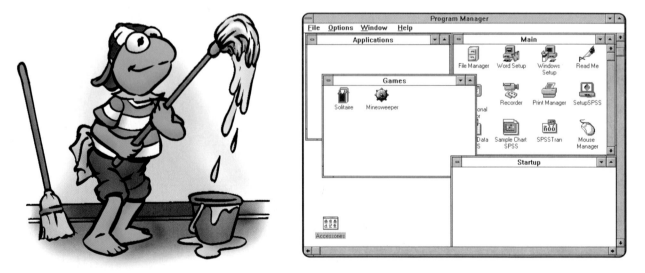

Just double-click on the little gray button with the minus sign in it [–]. Wow! The window disappears and the group icon suddenly appears at the bottom of the screen again.

Close all windows *except* the one that says
Program Manager in the title bar. Be careful not to
double-click on that one. If you do, all the windows
will close and you won't be able to play anymore.

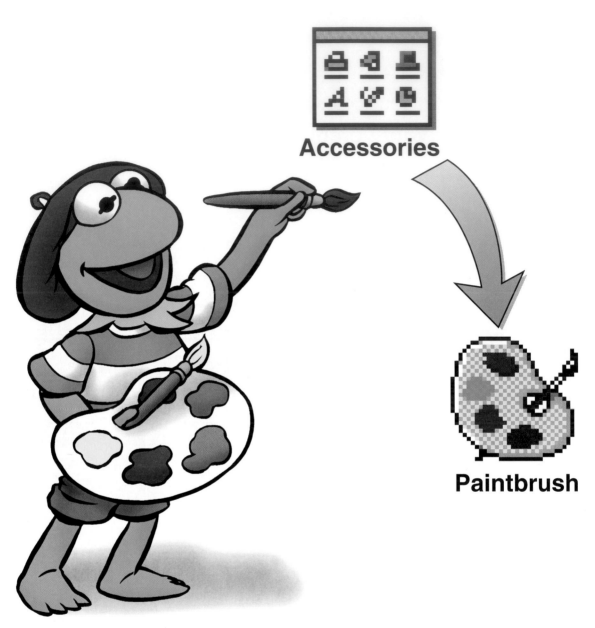

Accessories

Paintbrush

Now let's open my favorite program . . . **Paintbrush**! First we have to open the group window that stores the Paintbrush program. It's called **Accessories**. Move the pointer to the Accessories group icon. Double-click on it. There's the Paintbrush icon! Double-click on it. Presto! The Paintbrush window appears!

Scooter's Computer Tutor

It's okay if the name underneath the icon changes color and the window doesn't open. That just means that you single-clicked the icon. Keep double-clicking until the Paintbrush window opens.

I usually like to have more space to paint in. Scooter told me about some handy buttons that make windows bigger or smaller. You can see two of them now. They're those two little gray buttons ▼ ▲ on the Paintbrush title bar in the upper-right corner. Let's experiment!

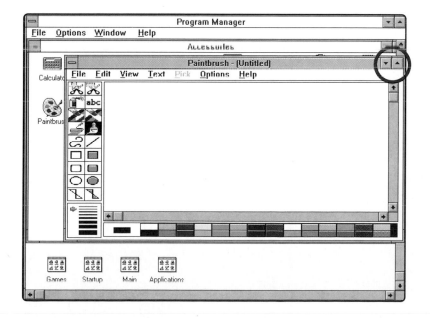

Click once on the button with the up arrow 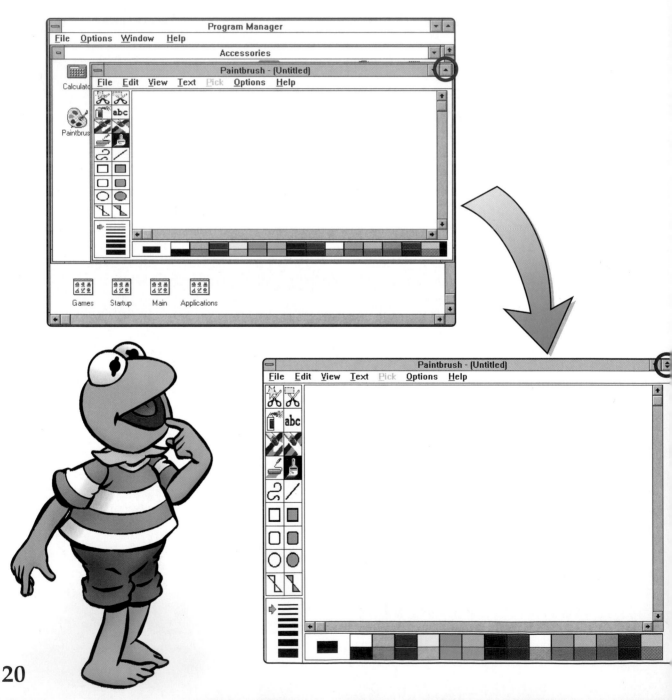 in it. Wow! Now the Paintbrush window fills the screen. Hey, look! The button in the corner now has two arrows in it that point up and down ⬍ at the same time. Weird.

If you click on that funny-looking up-and-down arrow button , the Paintbrush window shrinks back to the size it was when we opened it. And if you click on the down arrow button ▼, the window shrinks all the way back to an icon. Now you know how to make your windows any size you want!

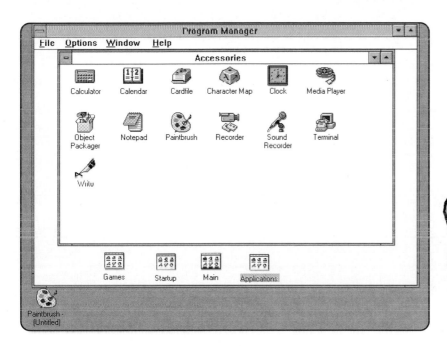

▲   This is called the **maximize button**.

▼   This is called the **minimize button**.

⬍   This is called the **restore button**.

Remember that if you shrink your window down to an icon, you just have to double-click on it to bring it back.

Okay, now let's get to the really fun stuff. I'm throwing a surprise birthday party for Piggy. And I need to make invitations to send to my friends. Do you want to help? We can create the invitations with the Paintbrush program.

Paintbrush - [Untitled]

File   Edit   View   Text   Pick   Options   Help

CLICK

Click on the up arrow button ▲ on the Paintbrush title bar to make the window really big if it isn't already. We're going to need a lot of space. The white part in the middle of the screen is where you draw and paint. It's like a blank piece of paper. On the left are your drawing and painting tools, and on the bottom are all the colors you can choose from. There are even fat lines and skinny lines.

23

Since this is an invitation to a birthday party, let's draw a cake, gifts, balloons, and streamers. How about starting with the cake? First, we need to choose a drawing tool from the **Toolbox**.

All you have to do is move the pointer to the Toolbox and click on the tool you want to use. Since we want to make a round cake, let's click on the **circle tool**. See how it turns dark? That means you've selected that tool.

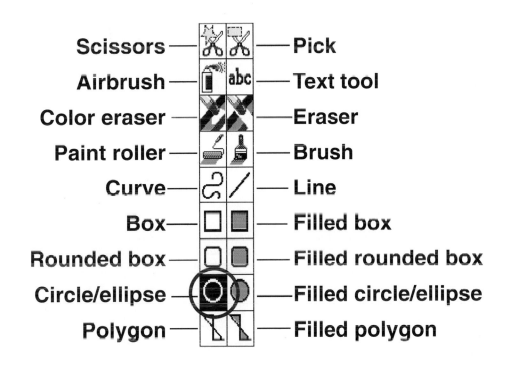

Scissors	Pick
Airbrush	Text tool
Color eraser	Eraser
Paint roller	Brush
Curve	Line
Box	Filled box
Rounded box	Filled rounded box
Circle/ellipse	Filled circle/ellipse
Polygon	Filled polygon

Scooter's Computer Tutor

Did you notice that there are two circle tools? That's because they do different things. The tool you just picked lets you draw empty shapes. The other circle tool lets you draw shapes that are filled in.

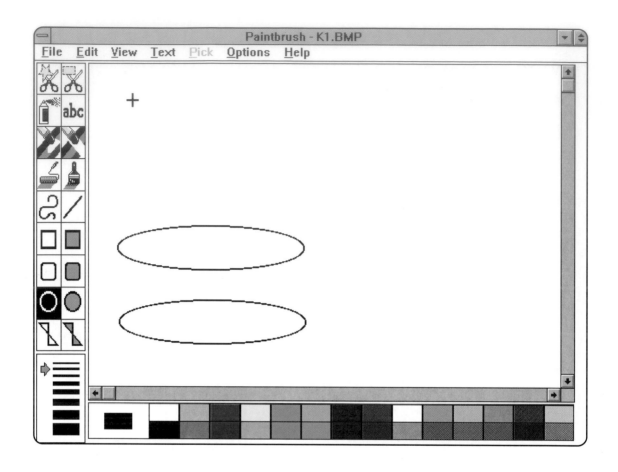

Now move the pointer into the drawing space. Did you see that? The pointer turned into a plus sign (+). Press and hold down the left mouse button and drag the mouse to the right and a little bit down. Lift your finger off the button. Look! You just made a squished circle! That's the top of the cake. Now make the bottom of the cake the same way.

Drawing on the computer is a lot different from drawing on paper, isn't it? But don't worry! If you make a mistake, you can make it go away. Just move your pointer to the top of the window. Click once on the word **Edit**. A menu will appear. Click on the word **Undo**. Your mistake will disappear! Piggy calls this the "Oops" command.

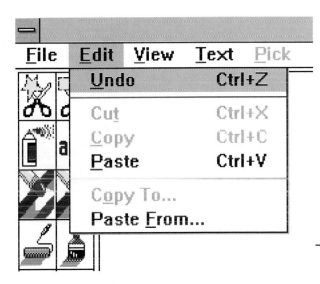

Scooter's Computer Tutor

You have to use the Undo, or "Oops," command right after you make a mistake or else it won't work. You can always erase your mistake if the Undo command doesn't work. Kermit will show you how on page 30.

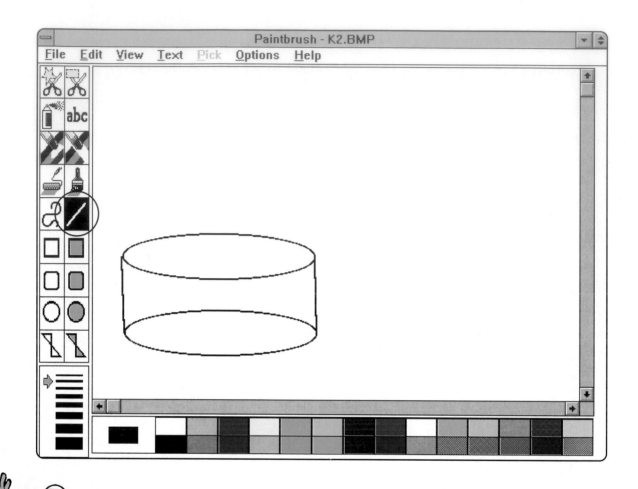

Next, let's make the sides of the cake. Click on the **line tool** in the Toolbox. Line up the center of the plus sign pointer with the top edge of the cake. Press and hold down the left mouse button. **Drag** the pointer to the bottom of the cake. Easy does it. See how the line follows the pointer? Lift your finger off the mouse button. Then do the same thing on the other side of the cake.

The cake has to sit on something. Let's make a plate for it. Go back to the Toolbox and click on the circle tool. Make another squished circle right under the bottom of the cake. It's got to be bigger than the bottom of the cake or the cake will fall off!

Do you want to get rid of any extra lines in the cake? Just click on the **eraser tool** in the Toolbox. Move the pointer over to the extra lines. The pointer turns into a little square (☐) this time. Press and hold down the left mouse button and drag the square over the parts you want to erase. Poof! They're gone!

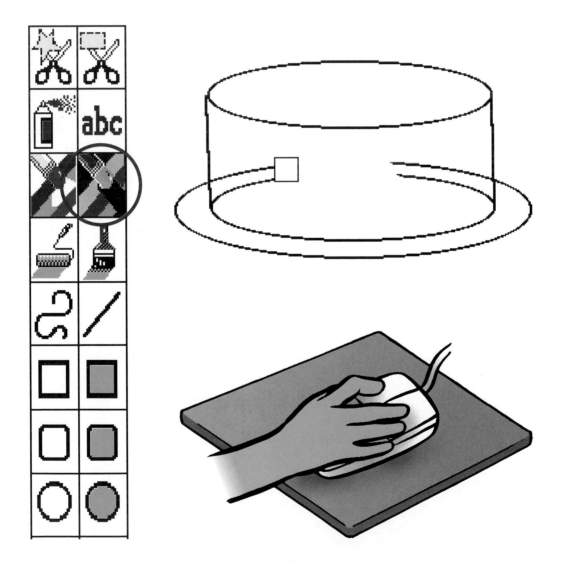

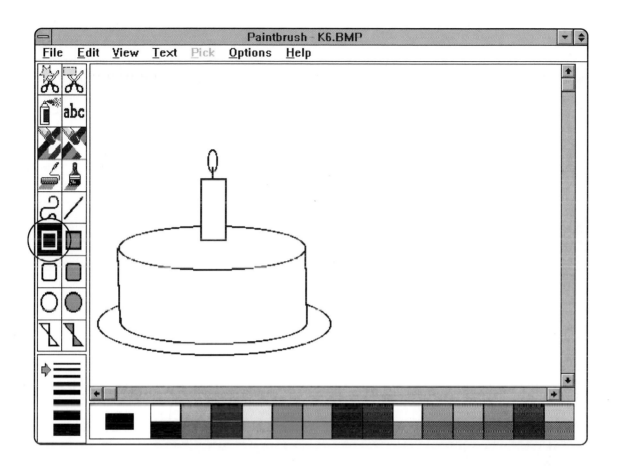

A birthday cake isn't complete without a candle, is it? This time click on the **box tool**. Make a tall, skinny box in the middle of the cake. Fool around with the pointer until you figure out how to make the candle shape. Now we've got to light the candle. Click on the line tool. Move the pointer just above the top of the candle. Draw a short line down to the top of the candle. That's the wick. To make a flame, click on the circle tool. Make a thin circle on top of the wick. Ta dah!

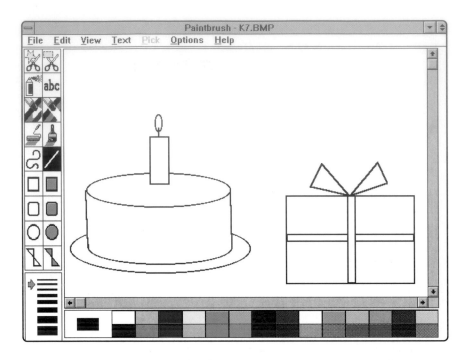

Can you make a gift for Piggy? Piggy loves gifts! Use the box tool to make the box and ribbons. You can make a bow by using the line tool. See how I did mine?

I used the circle tool to make these great balloons. Give it a try—it's fun. But now we need to tie strings to the balloons or else they'll float away! Use the **brush tool** to draw the strings.

linesize box

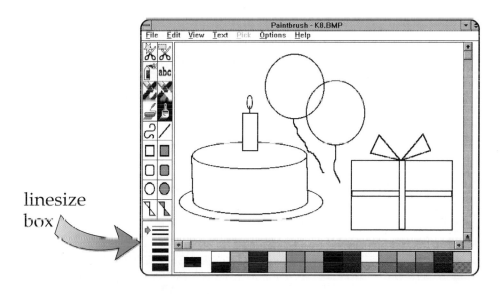

It's pretty tricky, so take your time. Just press and hold down the left mouse button and move the mouse around to make the string. Lift your finger off the mouse button when the string is long enough.

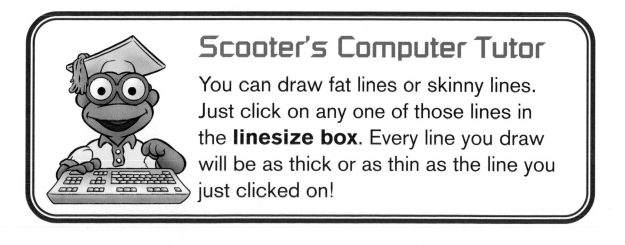

Scooter's Computer Tutor

You can draw fat lines or skinny lines. Just click on any one of those lines in the **linesize box**. Every line you draw will be as thick or as thin as the line you just clicked on!

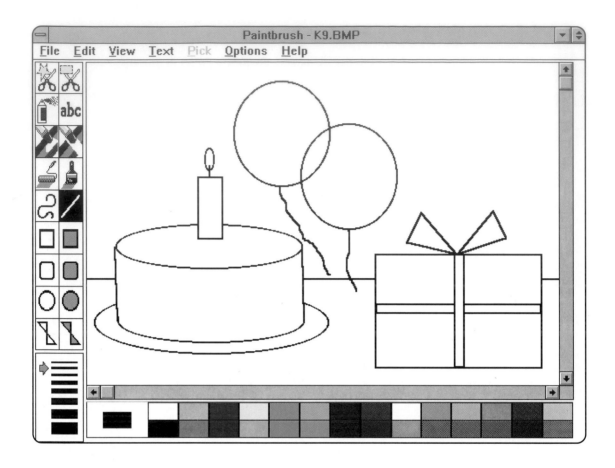

Now let's make a table for the cake and gift to sit on. Just click on the line tool. Put the plus sign pointer as far to the left as it will go. Draw a straight line all the way to the right. Don't worry, it's okay if the line goes through the cake or the gift. You can always erase those parts of the line with the eraser tool.

What a great picture! But it's missing something, isn't it? I know . . . it needs *color!* There are lots of colors to choose from right along the bottom of the window. That's your paint box, or **palette**.

Before you paint, you need to choose a brush. If you have a lot of space to cover, the way a house painter does, you select the **paint roller tool**. When you want to paint like an artist, you select the **brush tool**. And when you just want to have fun, try using the **airbrush tool**.

Let's try the brush tool first to make streamers. Click on the brush tool in the Toolbox. Then click on a color in the palette. Move the brush pointer to where you want to draw. Press and hold down the mouse button and drag the mouse around. Lift your finger off the mouse button when the streamer is long enough. Try different colors, too. Just click on a new color and draw more streamers.

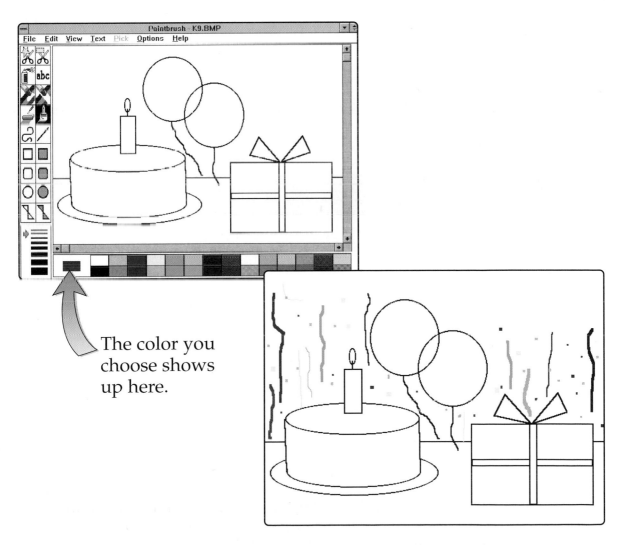

The color you choose shows up here.

37

Let's use the paint roller to color the cake. It paints big areas in a jiffy. Click on the paint roller tool and then click on brown. Move the paint roller over to the cake and click. Instant chocolate! Now color the rest of the picture.

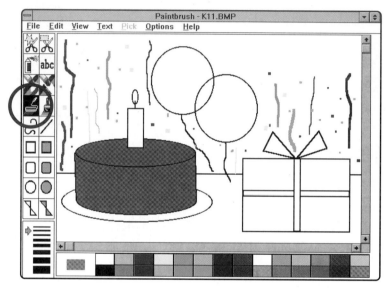

Be sure all the lines in your drawing are connected, or else the color will spill out.

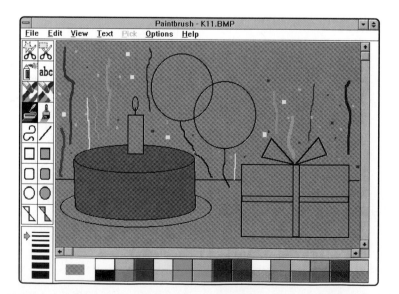

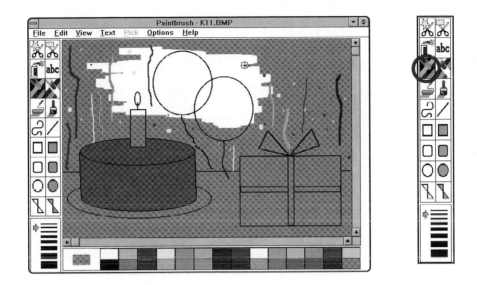

It's okay if colors leak out or if you don't like a color you chose. You can erase colors, too! Try the **Undo** command *right after* you make a mistake or if you change your mind about a color. If that doesn't work, try the **color eraser tool**. Click on the color in the palette that you want to erase. Click on the color eraser tool. Then click and drag the pointer over the part of the drawing that you want to erase. Only the color you clicked on will be erased!

Scooter's Computer Tutor

Let's fix that leak! Sometimes it's easier to just erase the unconnected lines and start all over again. But you can also simply fill in the hole. Click on the brush tool and move the pointer over to the leak. Then click and drag the pointer over the hole. Now, try to color it again. See . . . it works!

39

Let's add some words, too! Click on the **text tool** in the Toolbox. It's the one with **abc** on it. Click the color you want the letters to be. Move the pointer onto the drawing. The pointer looks like the letter **I** now! Click on the place where you want to start writing. Now use the keyboard to type this:

S U R P R I S E   P A R T Y !

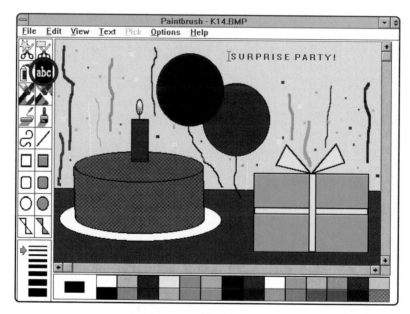

Scooter's Computer Tutor

To make capital letters, press the key that says [Caps Lock] before you type. To make an exclamation point, press and hold down the key that says [Shift] and type **!** at the same time. Did you get it? Good work! To make a space between the two words, press that long bar at the bottom of the keyboard. It's called the [Spacebar].

40

We need to print the invitations on pieces of paper so we can send them to our friends. Just move your pointer to the top of the window. Click once on the word **File**. Look—a menu drops down! Now click on the word **Print**.

You just opened the Print box. Click on the **OK** button in the box. Then just sit back and wait. Your printer does the rest of the work!

If you have a color printer, your invitations will print in color. If you don't, use paints or crayons to add your own special touch.

The screenshot shows a "Paintbrush - K15.BMP" window with a "Save As" dialog box open.

Save As

File Name: surprise

k1.bmp
k10.bmp
k11.bmp
k12.bmp
k13.bmp
k14.bmp
k15.bmp
k2.bmp

Save File as Type: 16 Color bitmap [*.BMP]

Directories: c:\muppets

c:\
muppets

Drives: c:

OK
Cancel
Info...

There! But we're not done yet. We have to save the picture if we want to see it again later. Click once on **File** at the top of the window. The same menu drops down. This time click on **Save**.

Another box opens. This is where you name your picture. Let's call it ⑤⓪⑧⑨⑨⑨⑧⑧⑧. Type in the name and click on the **OK** button with your mouse. Now your picture is saved on the computer!

If you want to come back to your drawing later, click on **File** to open the menu. Next, click on **Open**, and the Open box will appear. Below the words **File Name**, you will see a box that looks like this:

Put your pointer on the arrow that points down ⊞ and press on the mouse button. The file names will whiz by. Look fast! When you see your file, **surprise.bmp**, let go of the mouse button. Put your pointer on the file name and double-click. Your drawing will come back!

Scooter's Computer Tutor

You know how you should always put away your stuff when you're done playing? You should always close windows when you're done, too. Remember, close a window by double-clicking on the gray button with the minus in it ⊟ in the upper-left corner of the window you want to close.

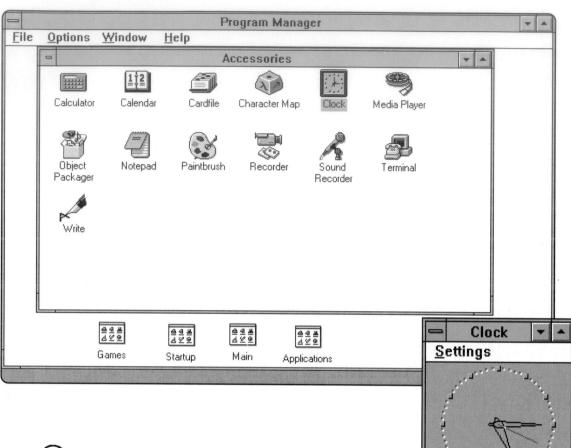

Gosh! I've been having so much fun, I wonder what time it is? Hey, did you know there's a special **Clock** window, too? Now, where is that clock? Oh, yeah, it's in the Accessories group window. Just click twice on the Clock icon and it pops right up. See? It tells you the time.

Watch this! If you click on the word **Settings**, a menu drops down. Let's see, I think I'd like to change it to a digital clock. I'll just click on **Digital** and . . . wow! It changed! It still says the same time, but it just says it in a different way. With this handy clock, I'll always know what time it is and I'll never be late. And speaking of late, I almost forgot! I have to go home. I'd better get going!

Just think of all the things we've learned together. We learned about icons, menus, and programs. We learned how to use a mouse. We learned how to open and close windows, and how to make them bigger and smaller.

And, best of all, we learned how to draw and paint on the computer. We even found a clock that tells us the time! And there are a lot more things we can do on the computer that we haven't even tried yet. But that will have to wait for another time. Until then, have fun exploring on your own!

A Special Note to Parents and Teachers

Kermit and the Muppet Kids welcome you and your child to the exciting world of Microsoft Windows! *Kermit Learns Windows* will help you explore the many wonderful things a computer can do, using one of the most popular programs available for the PC. With this book, your child will learn basic skills that will be useful for a lifetime. Before you begin this adventure in learning, here are the answers to some questions you may be asking yourself.

What Do I Need to Know?

The sample Windows screens that appear in the book assume that you have installed Windows according to the standard setup. If you have customized your Windows program or installed other programs that run under Windows, your screens may look somewhat different from those that appear here. Windows will work the same regardless.

Kermit Learns Windows also assumes that you already have Windows running when you begin. If you have not installed Windows or are unsure how to start the program, you may need to consult your manual. (*Windows 3.1: The Visual Learning Guide*, a full-color adult beginner's guide to Windows, is also available from Prima Publishing, either through your local retailer or by calling 1-800-255-8989, x504.)

It is extremely unlikely that your child could do anything to harm the computer while using the Windows software. If you have work files on the computer, you should, in any event, make backup copies of those files on a floppy disk to prevent accidental erasure. If at any time you become confused or the program seems to stop working, simply press the reset button on your computer to start over. Note that any drawings you have made with the Paintbrush program will be lost when you restart the computer unless you have already saved them.

How Do I Use This Book?

There are many new concepts and activities in this book. Mastering them all will take time and patience. Your child will have more fun if you keep things relaxed and offer lots of praise. There are no time limits or tests in this book. Feel free to break whenever you or your child needs to, and come back later.

Kermit Learns Windows should be read in front of the computer. It is an activity book, and your child will learn by doing as Kermit explains Windows with hands-on examples. Make sure your child is comfortable at the computer. The keyboard should be even with the elbows, the screen even with the eyes. Your child should be sitting up straight. The mouse should be held so the pointer finger rests on the left mouse button and the palm rests on the mouse.

If your computer is attached to a printer, you may wish to save your child's printouts and make them into a book. A three-hole punch and a simple three-ring notebook are all you need.

Where Do I Go Next?

Many schools offer computer education programs. In addition, there are a number of commercial enterprises that teach computers to children. Here's one:

Futurekids
5777 Century Blvd., Suite 1555
Los Angeles, CA 90045
1-800-PROKIDS

A number of companies offer educational software for children of all ages. For more information about the range of programs available, you may want to contact some of the companies listed below.

Broderbund Software, Inc.
500 Redwood Blvd.
Novato, CA 94948-6121
1-800-521-6263

Legacy Software
9338 Reseda Blvd., Floor 2
Northridge, CA 91324
1-800-532-7692

Davidson
P.O. Box 2961
Torrance, CA 90509
1-800-545-7677

Sierra On-Line
P.O. Box 485
Coursegold, CA 93614
1-800-326-6654

Disney Software, Inc.
500 S. Buena Vista St.
Burbank, CA 91521-6385

The Learning Co.
6493 Kaiser Dr.
Fremont, CA 94555
1-800-852-2255

For further reading, we suggest:

Kids & Computers magazine
A Magazine for Parents
Golden Empire Publications, Inc.
130 Chaparral Ct., Suite 260
Anaheim Hills, CA 92808
1-800-827-4450

Kermit Learns How Computers Work
  and *Windows for Teens*
Prima Publishing
P.O. Box 1260
Rocklin, CA 95677
1-800-255-8989, x504